MW00592727

DAY TRIPS ON
ST. MARTIN

by Robert Stone

Photographs by Robert Stone
Published by:
Day Hike Books, Inc.
114 South Hauser Box 865
Red Lodge, MT 59068
Copyright 1996

Distributed by:
ICS Books, Inc.
1370 E. 86th Place
Merrillville, IN 46410
1-800-541-7323
Fax 1-800-336-8334

TABLE OF CONTENTS

THE TRIPS

About St. Martin

DAY TRIPS on ST. MARTIN is a guide to the best beaches, quaint West Indian towns, historic forts, lush green hillsides and mountain peaks on this popular Caribbean island. St. Martin is located near the eastern portion of the Leeward Islands, 150 miles east of Puerto Rico and the U.S. Virgin Islands. Along the east coast of St. Martin is the Atlantic Ocean. On the west coast is the Caribbean Sea.

St. Martin is the smallest island in the world shared by two separate countries. The rural, northern portion of St. Martin is owned by France and encompasses 21 square miles of gorgeous coastline, rolling hills, farmland and quiet country roads. To the south is Sint Maarten, which is owned by the Dutch. It comprises 16 of the 37 square miles of this multi-national island. Although St. Martin is owned by two countries, there are no border formalities or custom checks except upon arrival to the island. French is the official language of St. Martin, and Dutch is the official language of Sint Maarten, but English is spoken everywhere. The same applies to currency. The U.S. dollar is accepted everywhere, even though the French franc is the currency of St. Martin, and the Netherlands Antilles guilder is the currency of Sint Maarten. Throughout the book, I will refer to the entire island as St. Martin for common English usage.

The weather on St. Martin is ideal. There is very little rain, and the temperature stays around 80 degrees throughout the year. Trade winds keep the humidity low and the air comfortably warm.

St. Martin offers duty-free shopping, gambling, the best cuisine in the Caribbean, superb accommodations, green mountains and more than 30 white sand beaches. With a fantastic selection of more than 300 restaurants—from bistros to haute cuisine—the hungry and adventurous diner can enjoy French, West Indian, Mexican, Italian, German, Indonesian, Thai, American and other international dishes.

Quelques Mots Sur Saint-Martin

DAY TRIPS on ST. MARTIN est un manuel d'itininéraires, d'une journée chacun, qui conduisent vers les plus belles plages, les villes les plus pittoresques, les forts historiques, collines luxuriantes et sommets de montagnes de cette île bien-aimée des Petites Antilles. Saint-Martin se situe près de la partie orientale des Iles Sous-le-Vent, 240 kilomètres à l'Est de Porto Rico et des Iles Vierges des Etats-Unis d'Amérique. L'océan Atlantique longe la côte Est de Saint-Martin, la mer des Antilles celle de l'Ouest.

Saint-Martin est la plus petite île du monde que deux pays différents se partagent. Sa partie rurale du nord appartient à la France et comprend 52 kilomètres carrés de littoral superbe, collines douces, terres agricoles et routes de campagne tranquilles. Au sud se trouve Sint Maarten, qui appartient aux Pays-Bas. La partie néerlandaise comprend 34 des 86 kilomètres carrés de cette île multi-nationale. Bien que Saint-Martin soit partagée entre deux pays, il n'y a pas de formalités à remplir ou de visites douanières à la frontière commune, en dehors de celles requises à l'entrée initiale de l'île. Le français est la langue officielle de Saint-Martin, tandis que le hollandais est celle de Sint Maarten, mais l'anglais se pratique partout. Il en va de même pour la monnaie. Le dollar des Etats-Unis d'Amérique est accepté partout, bien que le franc français soit l'unité monétaire de Saint-Martin et le "guilder" des Antilles néerlandaises celle de Sint Maarten. Tout au long du livre, j'utiliserai le nom de "Saint-Martin" quand je parlerai de l'île entière, pour simplifier.

Le climat de Saint-Martin est idéal. On y trouve très peu de pluie et la température demeure aux environs de 27° toute l'année, tandis que les vents alizés gardent l'humidité à son minimum et l'air tiède.

A Saint-Martin les achats sont exempts de droits. On y trouve le jeu, la meilleure cuisine des Antilles, des hôtels magnifiques, des montagnes verdoyantes et plus de 30 plages de sable blond. Grâce au choix extraordinaire de plus de 300 restaurants, allant de petits cafés à la haute cuisine, le dîneur cherchant l'aventure gastronomique trouvera excellents les plat offerts par la cuisine française, antillaise, mexicaine, italienne, allemande, indonésienne, thailandaise ou américaine entre autres.

✦ Beaches ✦

St. Martin has a beach for everyone. Along the island's scalloped coastline is a continuous series of bays, coves and unique beaches with easy access to swimming, snorkeling, diving, sailing, windsurfing, fishing, sunbathing and picnicking. Among St. Martin's varied beaches are those with long, open stretches of smooth, powdery sand, or beaches nestled in coves between rocks and palm tree-lined bays. There are popular beaches with watersport activities, or secluded clothing-optional beaches. Some beaches lie at the base of limestone cliffs with caves for exploring. Even more beaches can be found on offshore islands, cays and reefs. Boats are available for day trips to the neighboring islands of Anguilla, Nevis, Saba, St. Barts, St. Eustatius and St. Kitts for sailing, snorkeling, diving and exploring.

All of the beaches on St. Martin are open to the public, even when located on hotel property. Many beach-front hotels rent chairs, lounges and umbrellas.

✦ Driving ✦

St. Martin's main road circles the island, connecting both countries. The island can be circled by car in several hours, although you will want to linger at the various beaches and towns for a full day of exploring or relaxing. Rental car agencies calculate distance in either miles or kilometers. Distances in this book are given in both measurement systems. Driving is on the right side of the road. All foreign drivers licenses are valid on St. Martin.

Enjoy your holiday and day trips on St. Martin.

✦ Les Plages ✦

A Saint-Martin, chacun trouve la plage de son choix. La côte découpée de l'île est faite d'une série de baies, d'anses et de plages uniques propices à la natation, la chasse et la plongée sous-marines, la voile, la planche à voile, la pêche, le bain de soleil et le pique-nique. Parmi les diverses plages de Saint-Martin se trouvent celles au sable fin et poudreux, qui s'étalent sur de vastes longueurs, et les plages des anses, abritées d'un côté par les rochers et de l'autre par les palmiers qui longent les baies. On rencontre des plages en vogue où se pratiquent les sports nautiques ainsi que des plages isolées où les vêtements sont facultatifs. Certaines plages longent la base de falaises calcaires dont les grottes se prêtent à l'exploration. De nombreuses plages, enfin, se situent dans les îles, récifs et écueils au large de Saint-Martin. Des bateaux de plaisance mènent aux îles d'Anguilla, Nevis, Saba, St. Barts, St. Eustatius et St. Kitts pour une journée de voile, chasse ou plongée sous-marines ou encore la visite des environs.

Toutes les plages de Saint-Martin sont accessibles au grand public, même celles qui font partie de la propriété de certains hôtels en bordure de mer. Beaucoup d'entre eux louent des chaises, chaises-longues et parasols.

✦ Le Tourisme En Voiture ✦

La route principale de Saint-Martin fait le tour de l'île, reliant les deux pays. On peut faire ce trajet en voiture en quelques heures, mais vous voudrez peut-être vous attarder sur les différentes plages ou dans les villes, pour une journée de détente ou de découverte. Les agences de voitures de location calculent les distances soit en "miles", soit en kilomètres. Dans ce livre, les distances sont calculées aussi avec les deux systèmes de mesure. La conduite sur les routes est à droite et tous les permis de conduire étrangers sont valables à Saint-Martin.

Passez de belles vacances avec "Day Trips on St. Martin."

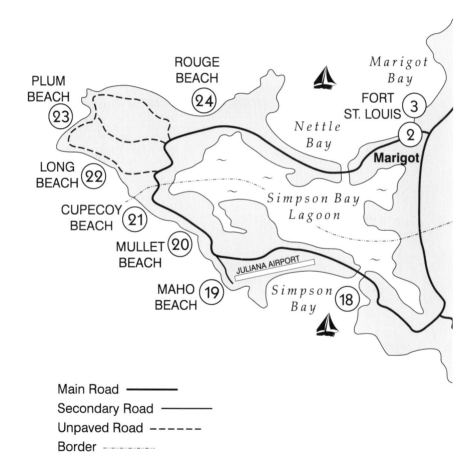

Caribbean Sea

ROUGE BEACH
(24)

PLUM BEACH
(23)

Marigot Bay

FORT ST. LOUIS (3)

(2)

Marigot

Nettle Bay

LONG BEACH (22)

CUPECOY BEACH (21)

Simpson Bay Lagoon

MULLET BEACH (20)

JULIANA AIRPORT

MAHO BEACH (19)

Simpson Bay

(18)

Main Road ———
Secondary Road ———
Unpaved Road ------
Border ----·-----

MAP OF

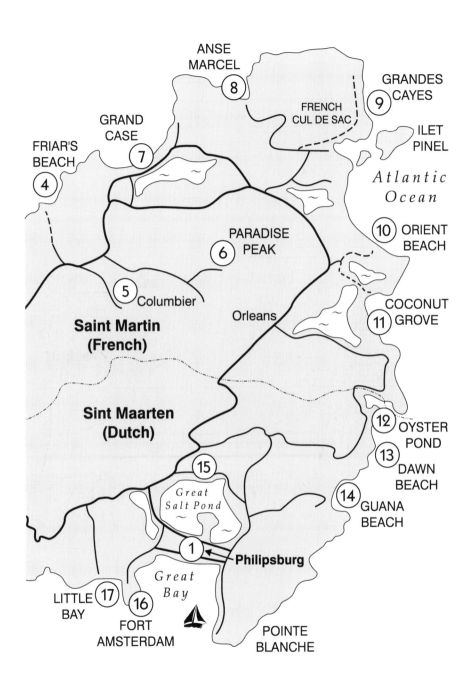

THE TRIPS

Trip 1
Philipsburg and Great Bay

Summary of area: Philipsburg, the Dutch capital of Sint Maarten, lies on the south end of the island on a narrow strip of land between the Caribbean Sea at Great Bay and Great Salt Pond. Two main streets, Front Street and Back Street, run through the town parallel to Great Bay with connecting lanes joining them. Philipsburg has renovated older buildings and ornate West Indian architecture with latticed eaves, porches and balconies. Many buildings are painted with lively Caribbean colors. This quaint village offers an historic town square, a museum, a beautifully restored courthouse built in 1793, duty-free shopping and a large variety of restaurants, hotels and gambling casinos. Be sure to stroll along Old Street, and view the colorful, restored buildings.

From the pier in the center of town are steps leading to the beach. Numerous alleyways along the length of Front Street also allow access to the one-mile stretch of beach. The sand is clean and the water is calm and clear. On the east end of the bay is a marina offering boats and ferries to neighboring islands.

Driving directions: From Marigot: Drive 2.6 miles (3.8 km) south on Rue de la Hollande (which becomes Union Road) towards Philipsburg to A.J.C. Brouwer Road. Turn left and continue 1.7 miles (2.9 km) to an intersection with a light signal and the Food Center Supermarket on the right. Turn right and drive 1.4 miles (2.3 km) east into Philipsburg.

The town of Philipsburg is small enough to comfortably cover on foot, so park wherever you find a spot.

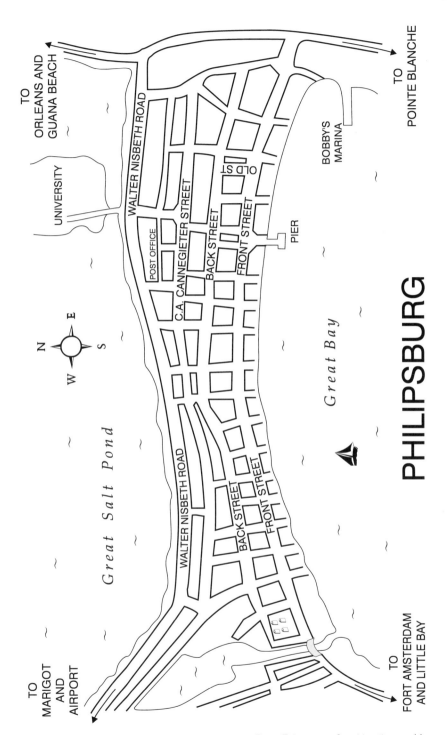

TO
ORLEANS AND
GUANA BEACH

TO
POINTE BLANCHE

TO
MARIGOT
AND
AIRPORT

TO
FORT AMSTERDAM
AND LITTLE BAY

UNIVERSITY

WALTER NISBETH ROAD

POST OFFICE

C.A. CANNEGIETER STREET

BACK STREET

FRONT STREET

OLD ST

BOBBY'S
MARINA

PIER

WALTER NISBETH ROAD

BACK STREET

FRONT STREET

Great Salt Pond

Great Bay

N
E
S
W

PHILIPSBURG

Trip 2
Marigot

Summary of area: Marigot, the French capital of St. Martin, is a charming harbor town located between Marigot Bay (Baie de Marigot) and Simpson Bay Lagoon. With casual atmosphere, outdoor cafes and bistros, European boutiques, the aroma of baked baguettes, warm croissants, cappuccino and outstanding French restaurants, Marigot is a delight.

Every Wednesday and Saturday morning, a colorful open-air market is held at the old marina on Marigot Harbor. Fisherman arrive to sell fresh fish, while local merchants sell tropical fruit, vegetables, spices, handcrafts and clothing. The weather is warm, the excitement is high, and you can stroll among buyers and merchants as they barter for prices and tell stories.

Driving directions: From Philipsburg: Drive 1.4 miles (2.3 km) west on Walter Nisbeth Road, which runs parallel to the Great Salt Pond, to an intersection with a light signal and the Food Center Supermarket on the left. Turn left and continue 1.7 miles (2.9 km) on A.J.C. Brouwer Road to the end of the road. Turn right onto Union Road and drive 2.6 miles (3.8 km) into Marigot. The town of Marigot is small enough to comfortably cover on foot, so park wherever you find a spot.

Additional note: A daily 10-minute boat shuttle will take you across Simpson Bay from the Pelican Resort, on the Dutch side, to Marigot for a day of sightseeing, people watching, shopping and French food.

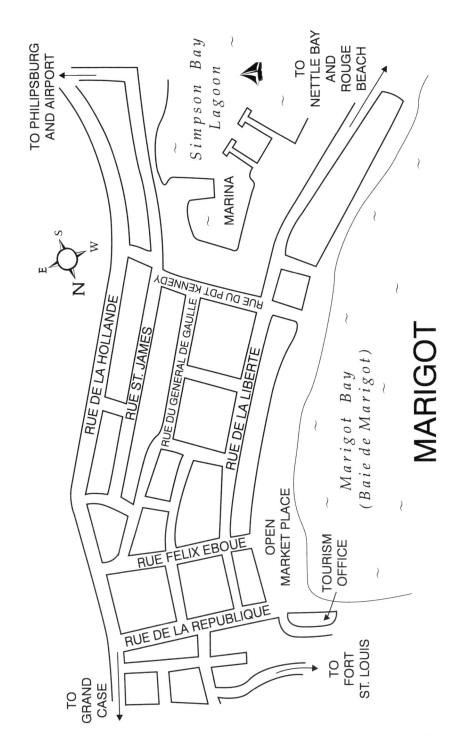

TO PHILIPSBURG AND AIRPORT

Simpson Bay Lagoon

TO NETTLE BAY AND ROUGE BEACH

MARINA

N E S W

RUE DE LA HOLLANDE

RUE ST. JAMES

RUE DU PDT KENNEDY

RUE DU GENERAL DE GAULLE

RUE DE LA LIBERTE

Marigot Bay (Baie de Marigot)

RUE FELIX EBOUE

OPEN MARKET PLACE

TOURISM OFFICE

RUE DE LA REPUBLIQUE

TO GRAND CASE

TO FORT ST. LOUIS

MARIGOT

Trip 3
Fort St. Louis
(Fort Marigot)

Hiking distance: 1.5 miles round trip
Hiking time: 45 minutes

Summary of area: Fort St. Louis, built in 1767 and recently restored, sits at the summit of a hill overlooking the city of Marigot, Marigot Bay, Simpson Bay Lagoon, the western portion of the island and the island of Anguilla in the Atlantic Ocean. The sweeping views are exceptional.

Driving directions: From Philipsburg: Drive 1.4 miles (2.3 km) west on Walter Nisbeth Road, which runs parallel to the Great Salt Pond, to an intersection with a light signal and the Food Center Supermarket on the left. Turn left and continue 1.7 miles (2.9 km) on A.J.C. Brouwer Road to the end of the road. Turn right onto Union Road and drive 2.6 miles (3.8 km) into Marigot. The hike begins by the Marigot Harbor. The fort is a short walk from anywhere in Marigot. If you wish to park close to the trailhead, park near the harbor.

Hiking directions: From Marigot Harbor, you can see Fort St. Louis by looking to the hilltop to the east. (See back cover photo.) Walk to the east end of the harbor. From this spot there are two accesses to the fort.

   1. Take the first alleyway from the harbor, and go up the stairs until the alley joins the fort road. Continue to the left, following the road which leads directly to the fort.

   2. From the east end of the harbor, walk inland along Rue de la Republique a short distance to Rue de l'Eglise. Turn left and continue one block to the Catholic Church. On the right side of the church is the street that leads to the fort.

Trip 4
Friar's Beach

Summary of area: Friar's Beach is located within a charming, picturesque cove by the Guichard Salt Pond inlet. This intimate beach has festive yellow, red and blue food stand cabanas and a tropical forest just beyond it. The bay offers excellent snorkeling.

Driving directions: From Philipsburg: Drive 1.4 miles (2.3 km) west on Walter Nisbeth Road, which runs parallel to the Great Salt Pond, to an intersection with a light signal and the Food Center Supermarket on the left. Turn left and continue 1.7 miles (2.9 km) on A.J.C. Brouwer Road to the end of the road. Turn right onto Union Road and drive 2.6 miles (3.8 km) into Marigot.

From Marigot: Drive 1.3 miles (2 km) northeast towards Grand Case to the Friar's Beach turnoff on the left. Turn left and continue 1 mile (1.6 km) along the winding road, past the residential homes, onto a gravel road. The road ends at the parking area for Friar's Beach.

Trip 5
Columbier

Summary of area: The trip through Columbier can be enjoyed as a beautiful two-mile walk or a scenic drive through rolling hills and green pastures along a quiet country road. Bordering the road are historic stone walls and lush flowering bougainvillea, hibiscus and poinsettias. With a backdrop of the northern mountains, you will view grazing goats and sheep and pass through the Creole village of Columbier. This area is highly recommended, as it is unique to any other location on the island.

Driving directions: From Philipsburg: Drive 1.4 miles (2.3 km) west on Walter Nisbeth Road, which runs parallel to the Great Salt Pond, to an intersection with a light signal and the Food Center Supermarket on the left. Turn left and continue 1.7 miles (2.9 km) on A.J.C. Brouwer Road to the end of the road. Turn right onto Union Road and drive 2.6 miles (3.8 km) into Marigot.

From Marigot: Drive 1.4 miles (2.3 km) northeast towards Grand Case to the Columbier turnoff on the right. Turn right. This 1.2 mile (1.9 km) road passes the charming village of Columbier at 0.7 miles (1 km).

Hiking directions: Only a few cars drive this road. The landscape, rock walls, flowers, goats, sheep and hills make it an enjoyable, picturesque walk. You may park anywhere along the roadside to begin your hike.

Along the road to Grandes Cayes - Trip 9

Overlooking Long Beach - Trip 22

Trip 6
Paradise Peak
(Pic Paradis)

Hiking distance: 1.2 miles round trip
Hiking time: 45 minutes

Summary of area: As the highest peak on the island of St. Martin—over 1400 feet—Paradise Peak offers sweeping views of the island, including both towns of Philipsburg and Marigot. Paradise Peak receives more rain than any other location on St. Martin. The lush vegetation makes for an exceptionally beautiful walk.

Driving directions: From Philipsburg: Drive 1.4 miles (2.3 km) west on Walter Nisbeth Road, which runs parallel to the Great Salt Pond, to an intersection with a light signal and the Food Center Supermarket on the left. Turn left and continue 1.7 miles (2.9 km) on A.J.C. Brouwer Road to the end of the road. Turn right onto Union Road and drive 2.6 miles (3.8 km) into Marigot.

From Marigot: Drive 1.7 miles (2.7 km) northeast towards Grand Case to the Pic Paradis turnoff on the right. Turn right and drive 1.2 miles (1.9 km) to an intersecting road on the left. (A direction sign is posted.) Turn left and continue 0.3 miles (0.5 km) to the parking area.

Hiking directions: From the parking area, continue up the road on foot. At the top of the hill are two magnificent lookout points. One looks east with views from Orient Bay to Philipsburg. The other looks west towards Marigot.

Trip 7
Grand Case

Summary of area: Grand Case, an historical fishing village, is located on the northeast side of the island. This quaint seaside village has charming Creole-style, West Indian architecture. Grand Case is rimmed by the Caribbean Sea on one side and green mountains on the other. It has one narrow main street and a beautiful beach. The quiet, mile-long white sand beach has calm, pristine water and excellent snorkeling along the south end.

On an island known for its gourmet food, Grand Case is known for the island's finest cuisine. Restaurants line the main road offering great food in a beautiful seaside setting. Try not to miss the opportunity to eat ribs, chicken or lobster from one of many local barbecue stands along the beach. The price is right and the flavor is worth savoring.

Driving directions: From Philipsburg: Drive 1.4 miles (2.3 km) west on Walter Nisbeth Road, which runs parallel to the Great Salt Pond, to an intersection with a light signal and the Food Center Supermarket on the left. Turn left and continue 1.7 miles (2.9 km) on A.J.C. Brouwer Road to the end of the road. Turn right onto Union Road and drive 2.6 miles (3.8 km) into Marigot.

From Marigot: Drive 3.8 miles (6 km) northeast towards Grand Case. Turn left at the Grand Case entrance road. This one-way road leads to the center of town, the coastline and eventually back to the highway. To the right are the hotels and beaches.

Red boat and green rock at Coconut Grove - Trip 11

Green pastures and rolling hills of Colombier - Trip 5

Gazebo on cliffs at Maho - Trip 19

Trip 8
Anse Marcel

Summary of area: Anse Marcel is another beautiful cove with calm water, surrounded on its sides by mountains that overlook the Caribbean Sea. A wide variety of watersports are available at this white sand beach. Boat excursions to neighboring islands leave from the marina. A spectacular country road leads to the marina and L'Habitation, a secluded resort which resembles a Mediterranean village. The hotel has shops, boutiques and restaurants.

Driving directions: From Philipsburg: Drive 0.7 miles (1 km) west on Walter Nisbeth Road, which runs parallel to the Great Salt Pond, to Illidge Road on the right. This is the first road that crosses the Salt Pond. Turn right on Illidge Road and drive to Zagersgut Road 0.4 miles (0.6 km) ahead. Turn right and continue 6.1 miles (9.8 km), passing through the town of Orleans, to the Cul de Sac/Anse Marcel turnoff on the right. Turn right.

From Marigot: Drive 5 miles (8 km) northeast, past Grand Case, to the Cul de Sac/Anse Marcel turnoff on the left. Turn left. This is the first left turn past the Grand Case Airport.

From the Cul de Sac/Anse Marcel turnoff: Drive 0.5 miles (0.8 km) to the Hotel Mount Vernon road junction. Take the left fork and continue an additional 0.5 miles (0.8 km) to the second road junction. Turn left again and drive up, over and around the hill for 1.1 miles (1.8 km) to L'Habitation Hotel. Park in the lot at the end of the road.

Additional notes: On the road to the bay, just before the parking area, is the Privilege Hotel on the left. For additional breathtaking views of the bay and surrounding area, take the steep road to the top. There are various scenic pullouts.

Trip 9
Grandes Cayes

Summary of area: Grandes Cayes is a majestic area with a rough, turbulent ocean. There is a coral barrier reef, which is great for diving, but it can be dangerous. You may park anywhere along the road and walk. Few cars drive this road, making it a superb area to hike and explore along the rock-lined shore.

Ilet Pinel and Petite Clef are tiny islands just off the coast. Both have beaches and coral reefs ideal for snorkeling. A short boat ride can be taken to either island from the Cul de Sac shoreline.

Driving directions: From Philipsburg: Drive 0.7 miles (1 km) west on Walter Nisbeth Road, which runs parallel to the Great Salt Pond, to Illidge Road on the right. This is the first road that crosses the Salt Pond. Turn right on Illidge Road and drive to Zagersgut Road 0.4 miles (0.6 km) ahead. Turn right and continue 6.1 miles (9.8 km), passing through the town of Orleans, to the Cul de Sac/ Anse Marcel turnoff on the right. Turn right.

From Marigot: Drive 5 miles (8 km) northeast, past Grand Case, to the Cul de Sac/Anse Marcel turnoff on the left. Turn left. This is the first left turn past the Grand Case Airport.

From the Cul de Sac/Anse Marcel turnoff: Drive 0.5 miles (0.8 km) to the Hotel Mount Vernon road junction. Take the left fork and continue an additional 0.5 miles (0.8 km) to the second road junction. (Straight ahead is the Cul de Sac shoreline.) Turn left and drive about 100 meters. Turn right onto the unpaved road just before the hill. This road follows along the north side of the Cul de Sac Marina and around the hill to Grandes Cayes. The road continues along the coastline for 1.3 miles (2 km) to the end of the road.

Arriving on St. Martin - Maho Beach - Trip 19

Fort St. Louis in Marigot - Trip 3

Sandstone cliffs at Cupecoy Beach - Trip 21

Trip 10
Orient Beach

Summary of area: Orient Beach is a famous and popular beach. The 1.5-mile crescent-shaped stretch of sand is best known as a clothing-optional "naturalist" beach, and is also popular with windsurfers. The turquoise waters are protected by a natural reef. The bay is an underwater marine reserve. Bars, restaurants and open-air clothing shops line the beach. Lounge chairs, umbrellas and watersport equipment are available for rent. The "naturalist" area is located on the southern end of the beach. A sign banning cameras, gawking tourists and radio/cassette players is posted. Please be respectful.

Driving directions: From Philipsburg: Drive 0.7 miles (1 km) west on Walter Nisbeth Road, which runs parallel to the Great Salt Pond, to Illidge Road on the right. This is the first road that crosses the Salt Pond. Turn right on Illidge Road and drive to Zagersgut Road 0.4 miles (0.6 km) ahead. Turn right and continue 4.6 miles (7.4 km), passing through the town of Orleans, to the Orient Beach turnoff on the right. Turn right.

From Marigot: Drive 6.5 miles (10.4 km) northeast, past Grand Case, to the Orient Beach turnoff on the left. Turn left.

From the Orient Beach turnoff: Drive 0.2 miles (0.3 km) and turn left onto an unpaved road. (Turning to the right leads to Coconut Grove, Trip 11.) Continue 0.5 miles (1.1 km) to the Orient Beach parking area.

Trip 11
Coconut Grove
(Baie de l'Embouchure)

Summary of area: Coconut Grove is a beautiful crescent-shaped bay, lined with trees and white sand shores, and protected by a reef. Located to the south of Orient Beach, this is an excellent windsurfing, snorkeling or just floating-on-a-raft beach. There are food services and watersport equipment rentals. Bathing suit tops are optional.

Driving directions: From Philipsburg: Drive 0.7 miles (1 km) west on Walter Nisbeth Road, which runs parallel to the Great Salt Pond, to Illidge Road on the right. This is the first road that crosses the Salt Pond. Turn right on Illidge Road and drive to Zagersgut Road 0.4 miles (0.6 km) ahead. Turn right and continue 4.6 miles (7.4 km), passing through the town of Orleans, to the Orient Beach turnoff on the right. Turn right.

From Marigot: Drive 6.5 miles (10.4 km) northeast, past Grand Case, to the Orient Beach turnoff on the left. Turn left.

From the Orient Beach turnoff: Drive 0.2 miles (0.3 km). Stay to the right, onto an unpaved road. (Turning to the left leads to Orient Beach, Trip 10.) Continue 0.6 miles (1 km) to the parking area.

Old Street in Philipsburg - Trip 1

View of Great Bay from Fort Amsterdam - Trip 16

Secluded cove at Cupecoy Beach - Trip 21

Overlooking Little Bay - Trip 17

Trip 12
Oyster Pond

Summary of area: Oyster Pond is located along the Atlantic Ocean on the east side of St. Martin. The beach, on the south side of the pond, has flawless white sand and boasts of excellent waves for body surfing. The area also has a protective coral reef and is popular for snorkeling.

Driving directions: From Philipsburg: Drive 0.4 miles (0.7 km) east on Walter Nisbeth Road, which runs parallel to the Great Salt Pond, to the end of the road. Turn left on Sucker Garden Road, and continue 1.8 miles (3 km) to the Dawn Beach/Oyster Pond turnoff on the right. Turn right and drive up, down and around this winding, hilly road 1.9 miles (3.1 km) to the Oyster Pond Beach Hotel to the right. Turn right and park in the hotel parking lot.

From Marigot: Drive 7.6 miles (12.3 km) northeast, past Grand Case and Orient Beach, to the Oyster Pond turnoff on the left in the town of Orleans. Turn left and drive 3.3 miles (5.4 km) to the Oyster Pond Beach Hotel to the left. Turn left and park in the hotel parking lot.

From the parking lot, walk past the swimming pool, along the walkway and to the beach.

Trip 13
Dawn Beach

Summary of area: Dawn Beach, located near the Dutch border on the east side of the island, has incredible sunrises each morning and is well worth the early wake up call and drive. The beach is a clean, wide stretch of white sand with coral reefs just off the shore that are superb for snorkeling. This is also a good swimming and windsurfing beach.

The drive to Dawn Beach goes up and over dramatic hills with incredible views of the windward coast.

Driving directions: From Philipsburg: Drive 0.4 miles (0.7 km) east on Walter Nisbeth Road, which runs parallel to the Great Salt Pond, to the end of the road. Turn left on Sucker Garden Road, and continue 1.8 miles (3 km) to the Dawn Beach turnoff on the right. Turn right and drive up, down and around this winding, hilly road 1.6 miles (2.6 km) to the Dawn Beach Hotel to the right. Turn right and park in the hotel parking lot.

From Marigot: Drive 7.6 miles (12.3 km) northeast, past Grand Case and Orient Beach, to the Oyster Pond turnoff on the left in the town of Orleans. Turn left and drive 3.6 miles (5.9 km) to the Dawn Beach Hotel to the left. Turn left and park in the hotel parking lot.

From the parking lot, walk past the swimming pool, along the walkway and to the beach.

Marigot Harbor on market day - Trip 2

Coral formations at Plum Beach - Trip 23

Trip 14
Guana Beach

Summary of area: Guana Beach is an isolated white sand beach located two miles east of Philipsburg along the Atlantic coast. The hilly road to Guana Beach offers some stunning views of Philipsburg. This secluded beach can have strong ocean currents—caution is advised when swimming. There are no food or sports facilities, so bring your own supplies.

Driving directions: From Philipsburg: Drive 0.4 miles (0.7 km) east on Walter Nisbeth Road, which runs parallel to the Great Salt Pond, to the end of the road. Turn left on Sucker Garden Road, and continue 0.4 miles (0.7 km) to Guana Bay Road on the right. Turn right and drive 1.2 miles (1.9 km) to the Guana Beach parking area on the left

From Marigot: Drive 9.3 miles (15 km) northeast, past Grand Case and south through the town of Orleans, to a junction at the end of the road. Turn right towards Philipsburg and continue 1.6 miles (2.6 km) to the Guana Bay Road on the left. Turn left and drive 1.2 miles (1.9 km) to the Guana Beach parking area on the left.

Trip 15
St. Maarten Zoo and Botanical Garden
Monday - Friday: 9 am - 5 pm
Saturday - Sunday: 10 am - 6 pm
Telephone: 32030

Summary of area: The St. Maarten Zoo and Botanical Garden is located north of the Great Salt Pond across from Philipsburg. Situated on three acres, this non-profit organization features animals, birds and plants native to South America and the Caribbean. Tropical birds are housed in two walk-through aviaries. There is also a petting zoo.

Driving directions: From Philipsburg: Drive 0.7 miles (1 km) west on Walter Nisbeth Road, which runs parallel to the Great Salt Pond, to Illidge Road on the right. This is the first road that crosses the Great Salt Pond. Turn right on Illidge Road and drive to Zagersgut Road 0.4 miles (0.6 km) ahead. Turn right and continue 0.5 miles (0.8 km) to a fork in the road. Take Arch Road, the fork to the right, 0.2 miles (0.3 km) to the zoo entrance on the right side.

From Marigot: Drive 2.6 miles (3.8 km) south on Rue de la Hollande (which becomes Union Road) towards Philipsburg to A.J.C. Brouwer Road. Turn left and continue 1.7 miles (2.9 km) to an intersection with a light signal and the Food Center Supermarket on the right. Turn right and drive 0.2 miles (0.3 km) to the Zagersgut Road/Bush Road junction. Take the left fork onto Zagersgut Road for 0.9 miles (1.4 km) to another fork in the road. Take Arch Road, the fork to the right, 0.2 miles (0.3 km) to the zoo entrance on the right.

Trip 16
Fort Amsterdam

Hiking distance: 3 miles round trip
Hiking time: 1.5 hours

Summary of area: Fort Amsterdam, the first Dutch fort in the Caribbean, was built in 1631. Shortly after being built, the Spaniards captured the fort, demolished the structure and returned the site to the Dutch in 1648. The remains of the fort as well as several cannons sit at the crest of a hill overlooking Great Bay, Little Bay and Philipsburg. The islands of Saba and St. Barts can also be seen from here.

Driving directions: From Marigot: Drive 2.6 miles (3.8 km) south on Rue de la Hollande (which becomes Union Road) towards Philipsburg to A.J.C. Brouwer Road. Turn left and continue 1.7 miles (2.9 km) to an intersection with a light signal and the Food Center Supermarket on the right. Turn right and drive 1.4 miles (2.3 km) east into Philipsburg. Park anywhere in Philipsburg. The hike to Fort Amsterdam heads west. The closer to the west end of Philipsburg you park, the shorter the hike.

Hiking directions: From downtown Philipsburg, walk to the west end of town along Front Street. Cross the bridge over Fresh Pond and continue up and over the hill on Little Bay Road. (Front Street becomes Little Bay Road upon crossing the bridge.) From this road you are able to see Fort Amsterdam on the point which separates Great Bay from Little Bay. Little Bay Road ends at Divi Beach Hotel. Stay to the left along the shoreline as the road passes the hotel and climbs a short distance to the decaying fort.

Trip 17
Little Bay

Summary of area: Little Bay, located west of Philipsburg and Great Bay, is beautiful. The Belair Beach Hotel and Divi Beach Resort are situated along this bay and joined by a beachfront walkway. Little Bay is ideal for strolling or jogging along the walkway or white sand beach. There are beachside bars and restaurants plus an excellent watersports facility. The water is clean, clear and calm. There is superb snorkeling along the east side of the bay.

Driving directions: From Philipsburg: Drive west on Back Street, running parallel to the bay two blocks from the water, to the end of the road at the west end of Philipsburg. Turn left and go one block to Front Street. Turn right on Front Street, which becomes Little Bay Road upon crossing the bridge. Drive one kilometer (less than a mile) to Divi Beach Hotel at the end of the road and park in the parking lot. Access to the beach is around the left side or through the hotel.

From Marigot: Drive 2.6 miles (3.8 km) south on Rue de la Hollande (which becomes Union Road) towards Philipsburg to A.J.C. Brouwer Road. Turn left and continue 1.7 miles (2.9 km) to an intersection with a light signal and the Food Center Supermarket on the right. Turn right and drive 1.2 miles (2 km) into Philipsburg. Turn right at the first opportunity in Philipsburg and drive to Front Street, the street running closest to Great Bay. Turn right on Front Street, which becomes Little Bay Road upon crossing the bridge. From here, follow the directions above.

Trip 18
Simpson Bay

Summary of area: Simpson Bay, located east of the Juliana Airport, is an excellent watersports area. The marina is an excursion center with tours leaving daily for the islands of Anguilla, Saba, St. Barts, St. Kitts and around St. Martin for snorkeling, diving, sailing and sightseeing. There is a daily boat shuttle to Marigot and a free boat shuttle crossing to the west side of Simpson Bay by the Royal Palms Hotel. Pelican Resort, on the east side of the bay by the marina, has a casino, white sand beaches, shell beaches, bars and restaurants. Across the highway north of Simpson Bay is the Simpson Bay Lagoon, the shortest route (via boat) to Marigot.

Driving directions: From Philipsburg: Drive 1.4 miles (2.3 km) west on Walter Nisbeth Road, which runs parallel to the Great Salt Pond, to an intersection with a light signal and the Food Center Supermarket on the left. Turn left and continue 1.7 miles (2.9 km) on A.J.C. Brouwer Road to the end of the road. Turn left onto Welfare Road and drive 1 mile (1.5 km) to Simpson Bay on the left. Turn left and park in the parking lot.

From Marigot: Drive 2.6 miles (3.8 km) south on Rue de la Hollande (which becomes Union Road) towards Philipsburg to the A.J.C. Brouwer Road/Welfare Road junction. Turn right and continue on Welfare Road 1 mile (1.5 km) to Simpson Bay on the left. Turn left and park in the parking lot.

Trip 19
Maho Beach

Summary of area: Maho Beach is a large and popular beach located at the west end of the Juliana Airport landing strip. Watching jets land overhead can be noisy, but fascinating. The pristine white sand and sparkling turquoise water are only a part of why Maho Beach is so popular. Next to the beach are a variety of quality restaurants, duty-free shops and gambling casinos. At both ends of the sandy beach are large rock formations. Along the south end is a walking path which meanders past tidepools. On the north end is the Maho Hotel with a walkway and gazebo overlooking the bay.

Driving directions: From Philipsburg: Drive 1.4 miles (2.3 km) west on Walter Nisbeth Road, which runs parallel to the Great Salt Pond, to an intersection with a light signal and the Food Center Supermarket on the left. Turn left and continue 1.7 miles (2.9 km) on A.J.C. Brouwer Road to the end of the road. Turn left onto Welfare Road and drive 3.4 miles (5.5 km) past the airport to the sea front. There is beach parking to the left. There is also parking to the right but it is crowded due to the Maho Hotel, shops and restaurants.

From Marigot: Drive 2.6 miles (3.8 km) south on Rue de la Hollande (which becomes Union Road) towards Philipsburg to the A.J.C. Brouwer Road/Welfare Road junction. Turn right and continue on Welfare Road 3.4 miles (5 km) past the airport to the sea front. From here, follow the directions above.

Trip 20
Mullet Bay Beach

Summary of area: Mullet Bay Beach is a magnificent stretch of white sand lined with palm trees in a postcard perfect setting. A boardwalk extends out to the sea along a rock garden on the south end of the beach for a romantic walk. From here you can view the island of Saba, count waves crashing against the rocks or watch surfers catching the waves. Sunsets from this boardwalk are especially beautiful. There are beachside bars and restaurants along this crescent-shaped bay. Watersports equipment and lounge chairs are available to rent.

Driving directions: From Philipsburg: Drive 1.4 miles (2.3 km) west on Walter Nisbeth Road, which runs parallel to the Great Salt Pond, to an intersection with a light signal and the Food Center Supermarket on the left. Turn left and continue 1.7 miles (2.9 km) on A.J.C. Brouwer Road to the end of the road. Turn left onto Welfare Road and drive 3.5 miles (5.6 km), passing the airport and curving to the right past the shops and restaurants of Maho and Mullet Bay. The beach parking lot is on the left.

From Marigot: Drive 2.6 miles (3.8 km) south on Rue de la Hollande (which becomes Union Road) towards Philipsburg to the A.J.C. Brouwer Road/Welfare Road junction. Turn right and continue 3.5 miles (5.6 km) past the airport to Mullet Bay. The beach parking lot is on the left.

Trip 21
Cupecoy Beach

Summary of area: Cupecoy Beach is unlike any other beach on the island. To the west of the main beach is a series of small, secluded coves, joined together by walking trails along the eroded sandstone cliffs overlooking the sea. Footpaths lead from the main trail down to the various coves. Some coves are clothing optional. This is a wonderful beach as well as a great place to explore coves, caves and hike along the trails.

Driving directions: From Philipsburg: Drive 1.4 miles (2.3 km) west on Walter Nisbeth Road, which runs parallel to the Great Salt Pond, to an intersection with a light signal and the Food Center Supermarket on the left. Turn left and continue 1.7 miles (2.9 km) on A.J.C. Brouwer Road to the end of the road. Turn left onto Welfare Road and drive 4.8 miles (7.7 km), past the airport and Mullet Bay, to the Cupecoy Beach public parking lot on the left. This parking lot is located just past the Sapphire Beach Club Hotel.

From Marigot: Drive 5.2 miles (8.4 km) west, past Nettle Bay, along the narrow strip of land between Simpson Bay Lagoon and the Atlantic Ocean. Continue to the Cupecoy Beach public parking lot on the right, just before the Sapphire Beach Club Hotel.

Trip 22
Long Beach
(Baie Longue)

Summary of area: Long Beach is a pristine crescent of unbroken white sand extending over a mile, edged with sandstone cliffs and the bluest of water. This secluded, top-optional beach has no food or watersport rental facilities. It is a quiet, large isolated beach, perfect for long walks, privacy and memorable sunsets over the water.

Driving directions: From Philipsburg: Drive 1.4 miles (2.3 km) west on Walter Nisbeth Road, which runs parallel to the Great Salt Pond, to an intersection with a light signal and the Food Center Supermarket on the left. Turn left and continue 1.7 miles (2.9 km) on A.J.C. Brouwer Road to the end of the road. Turn left onto Welfare Road and drive 5.6 miles (9 km), past the airport, Mullet Bay and Cupecoy Beach, to the turnoff on the left for Long Beach and La Samanna Hotel.

From Marigot: Drive 4.4 miles (7 km) west, past Nettle Bay, along the narrow strip of land between Simpson Bay Lagoon and the Atlantic Ocean. The Long Beach turnoff is on the right.

From the turnoff to Long Beach: Drive 0.7 miles (1.2 km) to the Long Beach parking area on the left side of the road. Follow the sandy path from the parking area through the trees to the beachfront.

Trip 23
Plum Beach
(Baie aux Prunes)

Summary of area: Plum Beach is a tree-lined, top-optional, secluded crescent beach of white sand and clear water. The dramatic "Bird Cliffs," coral formations on the north end of the beach, are worth exploring. There are no eating services so pack a picnic basket.

Driving directions: From Philipsburg: Drive 1.4 miles (2.3 km) west on Walter Nisbeth Road, which runs parallel to the Great Salt Pond, to an intersection with a light signal and the Food Center Supermarket on the left. Turn left and continue 1.7 miles (2.9 km) on A.J.C. Brouwer Road to the end of the road. Turn left onto Welfare Road and drive 6.2 miles (10 km), past the airport, Mullet Bay and Cupecoy Beach, to the turnoff on the left for Plum Beach. I know this sounds fruity, but the turnoff sign says "Baie aux Prunes."

From Marigot: Drive 3.7 miles (6 km) west, past Nettle Bay, along the narrow strip of land between Simpson Bay Lagoon and the Atlantic Ocean. The Plum Beach turnoff is on the right. The turn is marked with a "Baie aux Prunes" sign.

From the turnoff to Plum Beach: Drive 1.2 miles (1.9 km) to a road junction. Take the road which curves to the right for 0.2 miles (0.3 km) to the parking area for Plum Beach. From the parking area, walk to the beach along a fence-lined access trail.

Trip 24
Rouge Beach
(Baie Rouge)

Summary of area: Rouge Beach is a large, beautiful expanse of clean, white sand and clear aquamarine water in a secluded cove (cover photo). The diving and snorkeling around David Hole, at the north end of the beach, is superb. This top-optional beach is considered to be among the most beautiful beaches on St. Martin. There are coral formations, caves, tropical vegetation, picturesque gazebos and a cabana serving refreshments. Lounge chairs and umbrellas are available to rent.

Driving directions: From Philipsburg: Drive 1.4 miles (2.3 km) west on Walter Nisbeth Road, which runs parallel to the Great Salt Pond, to an intersection with a light signal and the Food Center Supermarket on the left. Turn left and continue 1.7 miles (2.9 km) on A.J.C. Brouwer Road to the end of the road. Turn left onto Welfare Road and drive 7.1 miles (11.5 km), past the airport, Mullet Bay and Cupecoy Beach, to the Rouge Beach parking area on the left side of the road.

From Marigot: Drive 2.9 miles (4.6 km) west, past Nettle Bay, along the narrow strip of land between Simpson Bay Lagoon and the Atlantic Ocean. The Rouge Beach parking area is on the right side of the road.

Taxi Fares
(as of September 1995)

For a taxi or taxi information, phone:
22359
44248
54317

		Rates from Philipsburg	Rates from Juliana Airport
To:	Anse Marcel	$25	$30
	Columbier	12	12
	Cul de Sac	18	20
	Cupecoy Beach	12	8
	Dawn Beach	12	18
	Friar's Beach	12	12
	Grand Case	16	16
	Great Bay	—	10
	Little Bay	4	8
	Long Beach	16	10
	Maho Beach	10	5
	Marigot	8	8
	Mullet Bay	10	5
	Orient Beach	15	20
	Orleans	10	15
	Oyster Pond	15	20
	Philipsburg	—	10
	Simpson Bay	8	5

St. Martin Tourism Offices

In Philipsburg:
Walter Nisbeth Road 23
(3rd floor)
Tel: (5995) 22337
Fax: (5995) 22734
Chamber of Commerce
Tel: 23590 or 22088

In Marigot:
Located by the waterfront
Tel: (590) 87-57-21 or 87-53-26
Fax: (590) 87-56-43

In the United States:
Sint Maarten Tourist Office
275 7th Ave. (19th floor)
New York, NY 10001-6708
(212) 953-2084

French Gov't. Tourist Office
610 5th Ave.
New York, NY 10020
Tel: (900) 990-0040
    (212) 757-1125
Fax: (212) 247-6468

Information Sources

Juliana Airport - Phone 44224 or 54211
Flight Information - 52161
American Airlines - Phone 42040

Police
Philipsburg - Phone 22222 or 22112
Located behind post office

Marigot - Phone 87-88-33 or 87-50-06
Located on Rue de la Hollande

Ambulance
Philipsburg - Phone 22111 or 13011
Marigot - Phone 87-86-25 or 86-72-00

United States Embassy - Phone 61-30-66

American Express - Phone 22678

Other Day Hike Guidebooks

___ Day Hikes on Oahu $6.95
___ Day Hikes on Maui 6.95
___ Day Hikes on Kauai 6.95
___ Day Trips on St. Martin 9.95
___ Day Hikes in Denver 6.95
___ Day Hikes in Boulder, Colorado 6.95
___ Day Hikes in Steamboat Springs, Colorado 6.95
___ Day Hikes in Summit County, Colorado
      Breckenridge, Dillon, Frisco, Keystone, and Silverthorne . 6.95
___ Day Hikes in Aspen, Colorado 7.95
___ Day Hikes in Yellowstone National Park
      25 Favorite Hikes 7.95
___ Day Hikes in the Grand Tetons and Jackson Hole 7.95
___ Day Hikes in Los Angeles
      Venice/Santa Monica to Topanga Canyon 6.95
___ Day Hikes in the Beartooths
      Red Lodge to Cooke City, Montana 4.95

These books may be purchased at your local bookstore or they will be glad to order them. For a full list of titles available directly from ICS Books, call toll-free 1-800-541-7323. Visa or Mastercard accepted.

- -

Please include $2.00 per order to cover postage and handling. Please send the books marked above. I enclose $ _____

Name _____

Address _____

City _____ State _____ Zip _____

Credit Card # _____ Exp. _____

Signature _____

1-800-541-7323

46 - Day Trips on St. Martin

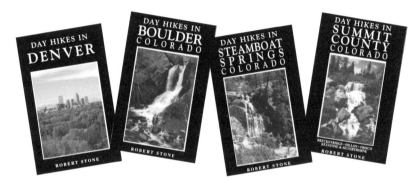
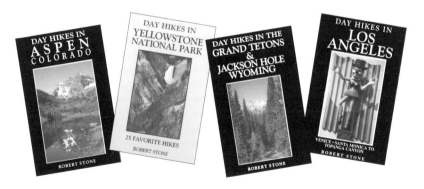

LINDA BOWER

ABOUT THE AUTHOR

A repeat traveler to St. Martin for many years, Robert Stone has a special appreciation for the opportunity to spend part of every winter in the warmth of the Caribbean.

Robert has traveled, hiked, and photographed extensively throughout Asia, Europe, the Caribbean, Hawaiian Islands and the Continental United States. When not traveling, Robert makes his home in the Rocky Mountains of Montana near Yellowstone National Park.